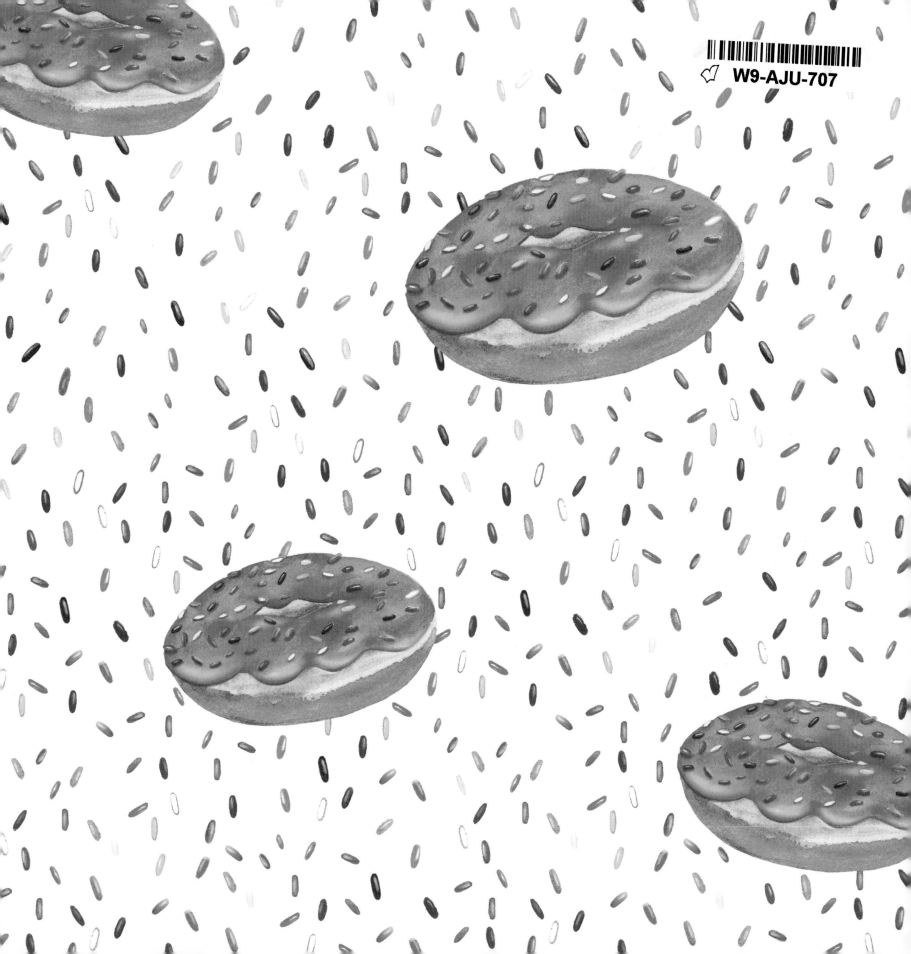

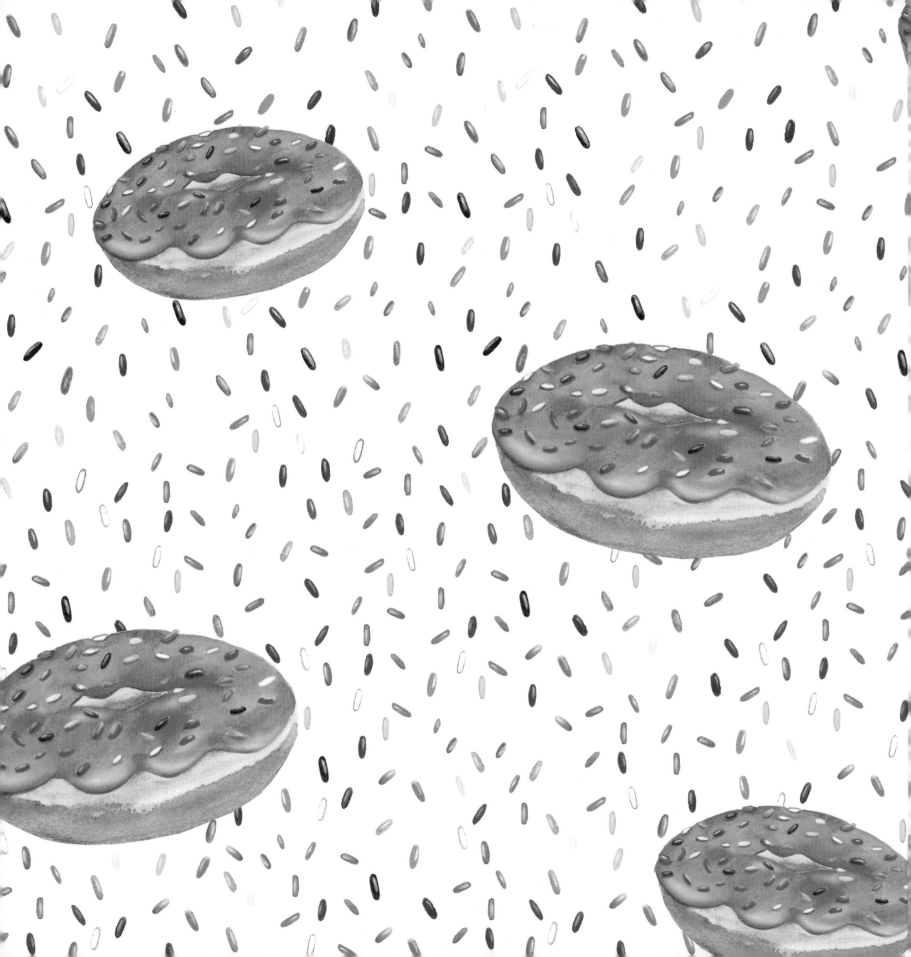

TO:

....

FROM:

....

DATE:

....

For Gina Williams, in celebration of ten years of service to the children of Oak Hills Church

I'm Not a Scaredy-Cat

© 2017 by Max Lucado

Published in Nashville, Tennessee, by Tommy Nelson. Tommy Nelson is an imprint of Thomas Nelson. Thomas Nelson is a registered trademark of HarperCollins Christian Publishing, Inc.

Illustrated by Shirley Ng-Benitez

Tommy Nelson titles may be purchased in bulk for educational, business, fund-raising, or sales promotional use. For information, please e-mail SpecialMarkets@ThomasNelson.com.

ISBN-13: 978-0-7180-7491-3

Library of Congress Cataloging-in-Publication Data

Names: Lucado, Max, author. | Ng-Benitez, Shirley, illustrator.
Title: I'm not a scaredy-cat : a prayer for when you wish you were brave / by
   Max Lucado ; illustrated by Shirley Ng-Benitez.
Description: Nashville : Thomas Nelson, 2017.
Identifiers: LCCN 2017000876 | ISBN 9780718074913 (jacketed hardcover)
Subjects: LCSH: Children--Religious life--Juvenile literature. |
   Fear--Religious aspects--Christianity--Juvenile literature. | Fear in
   children--Juvenile literature.
Classification: LCC BV4571.3 .L835 2017 | DDC 270.083--dc23 LC record available at https://lccn.loc.gov/2017000876

Printed in China

17 18 19 20 DSC 6 5 4 3 2 1

Mfr: DSC / Shenzhen, China / October 2017 / PO 9449357

I'm Not a SCAREDY CAT

A Prayer for When You Wish You Were Brave

MAX LUCADO

ILLUSTRATED BY SHIRLEY NG-BENITEZ

Tommy NELSON®

A Division of Thomas Nelson Publishers

Dear Mom and Dad,

Childhood fears. We all had them. When I was six years old, my dad let me stay up with the rest of the family and watch the movie *Wolfman*. Boy, did he regret that decision. The film left me convinced that Wolfman spent each night prowling our den, awaiting his preferred meal of first grade, red-headed, freckle-salted boy. My fear proved problematic. To reach the kitchen from my bedroom, I had to pass perilously close to his claws and fangs, something I was loath to do. More than once, I retreated to my father's bedroom and awoke him. Like Jesus in the boat, Dad was sound asleep in the storm.

How can a person sleep at a time like this? Opening a sleepy eye, Dad asked to be reminded, "Now, why are you afraid?" And I would remind him of the monster. "Oh, yes, the Wolfman," he'd grumble. He would then climb out of bed, arm himself with superhuman courage, escort me through the valley of the shadow of death, and pour me a glass of milk.

That's what parents do. We help our children face their fears. We can't remove all the sources of angst, but we can prepare our children to face them. As we give them tools to face the fears of childhood, we are actually preparing them to face the anxieties of adulthood.

I wrote this simple story to help children face their fears. I'm praying that you will find it to be a helpful tool. May God use it, and use you, to instill a godly bravery in the heart of your child.

MAX LUCADO

I'm a big cat. I'm a strong cat.

I'm not a **scaredy-cat** . . . except when . . .

My rubber ducky squeaked.

Oh my, how I freaked!

I gave it a squeeze and, as loud as you please,

It let out a **GREAT**

BIG

"EEK!"

The band on the street
Played **"tweet-a-tweet-tweet."**

They marched in their suits
    and tooted their flutes.
I nearly jumped out of my feet.

Has it happened to you?

Here is what *I* do.

When noises are loud or I feel lost in the crowd,

I say, "**God, can I talk to you?**"

I'm a big cat. I'm a strong cat.

I'm not a **scaredy-cat** . . . except when:

The monkey in the cabana
   Grabbed the yellow banana.
I hid under the table, in case he was able
   To reach my **bright**
   blue
   bandana.

A leaf from a tree
    Landed right on my knee.
I jumped with a **bump**,
    fell down with a

thump–

And that's what happened to me.

The slide's tippy-top
Made my tummy **flippy-flop**.
High above all, I tried not to bawl.

**What if
I couldn't
STOP?**

It's frightening out there,
  And new things can scare.
When you feel queasy, **oh so uneasy**,
  May I suggest this prayer?

Then you'll feel better.

I'm a big cat.
I'm a strong cat.
I'm not a **scaredy-cat** . . .
except when:

The elephant at the zoo

Sneezed a ginormous **ah-CHOO!**

I turned and I ran and hid in a can.

I did not know what to do!

The caterpillar, **all furry**,

Crawled on my foot, in no hurry.

He sat and he stared. He hadn't a care.

But my, how he made me

WORRY.

Are you ever afraid?
If so, **that's OK**.
When you feel frantic,
there's no need to panic.
Just turn to God and say:

"God, you are good.
God, you are near.
God, you are here!
And, God, you love me."

And you'll feel better.

I'm a big cat. I'm a strong cat.

I'm not a **scaredy-cat** . . . except when:

The baker in the store
Threw **sprinkles** galore!
Yellow and **pink**! I shuddered to think
The baker might sprinkle some more.

TICK

TOCK

TICK TOCK

The clock **ticked** and **tocked**.
I let out a **SQUAWK!**
I covered my ears and fought back the tears.
I admit, I was afraid of a clock.

The rain made a **splatter**,
A **splash**, then a **CLATTER**.
My fur was all wet. I started to fret.
Getting soaked is no laughing matter.

Next time you feel fearful,

All skittish and tearful,

Take time to pray—I know what to say

To make you feel **happy**
and **cheerful** . . .

"God, you are good.
God, you are near.
God, you are here!
And, God,
YOU LOVE ME."

Then you'll
feel better.

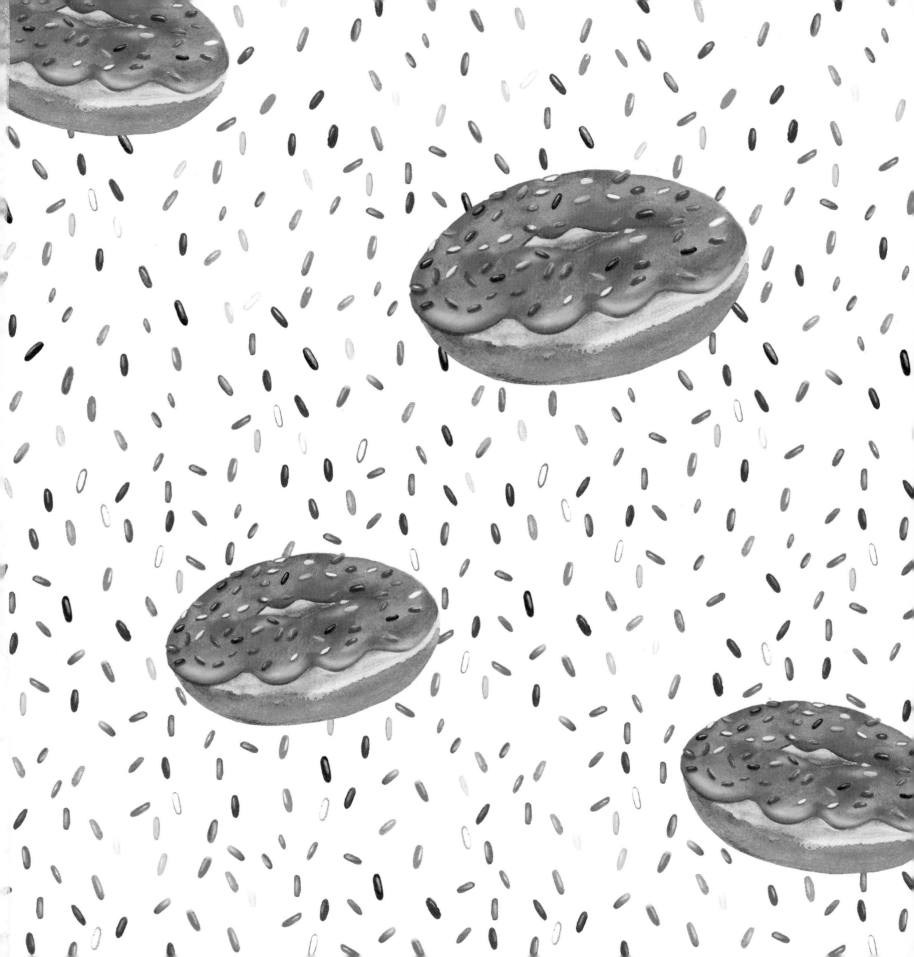

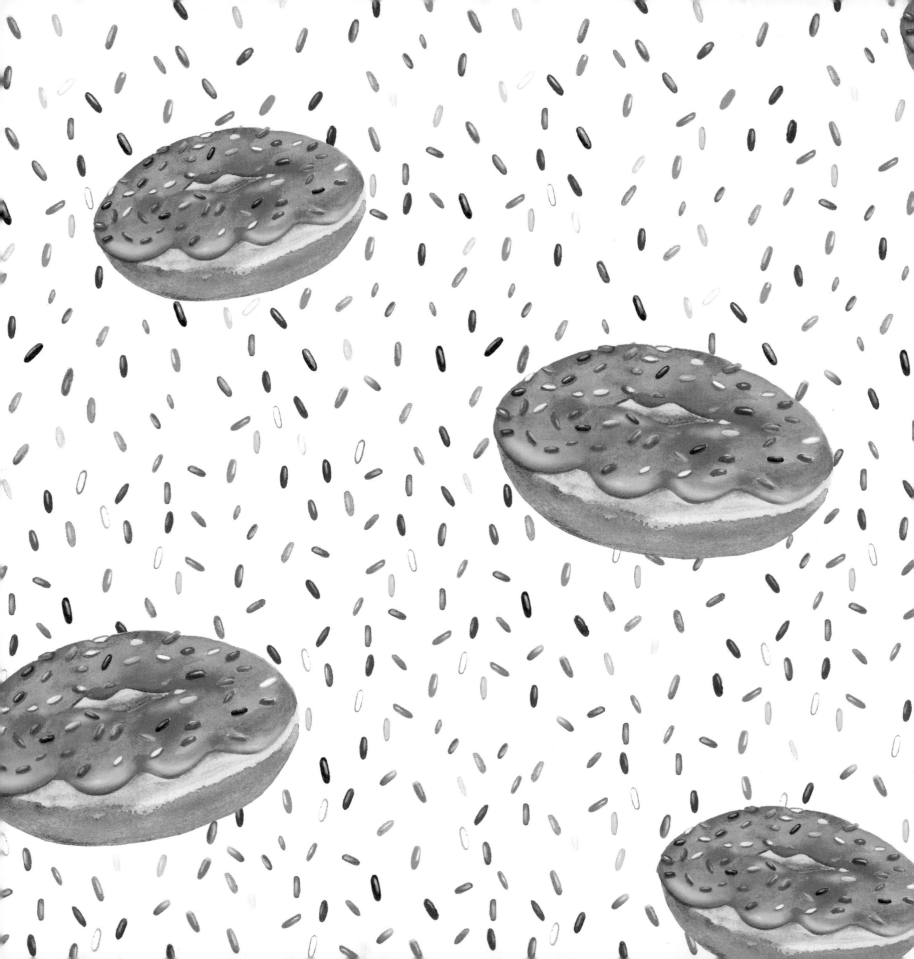